BENEATH THE MIDNIGHT SKY

POETRY OF LOVE'S TRIALS AND TRIUMPHS

KUNAL GARG

Contents

Beneath The Midnight Sky

A collection of poems taking you on a journey back in time, with every emotion experienced like love, temptation, heartbreak, and even loneliness; all brought to life in a string of beautiful words.

Introduction

Beneath the midnight sky - Poetry of Love's trials and triumphs is not just a collection of poems written over time, but they are a journey back in time, which resonates with each individual somewhere.

We all share experiences in our lives, which begins with choosing a family outside our own blood relations called friends, or the extended family. Drifting further, we fall in love, go through heartbreaks, fall for temptation, and even let the loneliness from such bonds seep in our very lives, only to rise again and repeat the cycle of life. These emotions are the various masks that every heart is known to wear throughout their life.

Falling and rising back again with each situation in life is the vicious cycle we all go through. Beneath the midnight sky - Poetry of Love's trials and triumphs may not just be a peek into my life alone; instead, it could be a journey back into your past life too!

Hope you connect with me on every page and find yourself hidden somewhere around the corner, waiting for a revival!

1. Special Friends

I've always seen my life as a journey on a road to tomorrow
There have been hills & valleys and turns here & there
that have filled my life with all kinds of challenges and changes.

But I made through those times,
'cause there were always special friends
I met along the way.

My special friends are the ones, who've walked beside me,
comforting my spirit or holding my hand
when I needed it the most.

They were friends who loved my smiles
and were not afraid of my tears.
They were true friends who really cared about me.
Those friends are forever;
They're cherished and loved more than they'll ever know.

You're one of my special friends
and a beautiful part of my life!!

2. Love

Love is when you really care about someone.
Love is when your time for "sweet-hearting" others is done.
Love is when no one else in the world could ever take your place,
love is when all the memories of things you do can't be erased.

Love is when you're crying after you and your man had a fight.
Love is when you really don't want your man in sight.
Love is when you can't see your man, so they're a big miss.
Love is when you really need some affection and a li'l kiss.

Love is when you whisper something sweet in your man's ear,
especially those three words they like to hear.
Love is when you will do anything for your man,
love is when other really start to "player-hate".

Love is when you can't put that person off your mind,
because that's the person you've always dreamt you'd find.
Love is when you're both happy together.
Love is when nothing in this world but you really matter.

Love is like a burning flame that will last eternally.
Love is when your feelings are locked-up and that
person has the key.

Love is when you seems to be diving in
a sky blue ocean.
If you think deep about it, you can really
feel the motion.

3. Don't Fall In Love

Have you ever fallen in love,
but knew they did not care?
Have you ever felt like crying,
but knew you'd get nowhere?
Have you ever watched 'em walk away...
not wanting them to go?
And whispered, "I Love You" softly...
not wanting them to know?
You cried all night in a misery,
and almost went insane.
There's nothing in this world
that causes so much pain.
If I could choose between love and death,
I think I'd rather die.
Love is fun, but it hurts too much
and the price you pay is high.
So I say, Don't Fall In Love,
for you'll be hurt before it's through.
You see my friend I ought to know,
I fell in love with you.

4. Hot Pink

All night long,
I thought about you.
I'm even dreaming while awake,
lost to hot pink thoughts of you.
No matter where I go,
no matter how near or how far,
I can't stop hearing
the beat of your heart.
I can picture us together,
in a field of hot pink irises.
I can feel the heat
and the power of our passion.
As you take me into your arms,
the world fades around us,
and I'm lost to the taste of
your sweet lips.
My fever for you
is burning me up inside.
I can see us...
you and I.
As the night falls,
so cold and dark,
I'll be thinking of you again.
I'd drive all night to reach you.
And when I'd found you at last,

I'd creep into your room,
and make love to you.
Nothing can cool this heat
I have for you.
Nothing you can say or do
will make these hot pink
fantasies fade.

5. We Are Friends

We've shared our happiness
And our dreams.
We've opened up to each other
To reveal what's in our heads.
We've talked about our fears,
Our hopes,
And everything in between.
We know each other so well
That we can sense
Each other's sadness
And feel each other's joy.
We've laughed together,
And we've cried together.
And we've never stopped
Believing in each other,
And wishing each other
The best life has to offer.
We trust each other completely
And know that we can depend on
Each other come the worst weather.
We are friends,
And for that, I am grateful!

6. Love For A Friend

I feel my heart breaking in two,
He doesn't love me as he loves you.
I thought maybe, someday.
But now it seems like never, no way.

I act like I don't care, but I'm new to these matters.
I hear of them together, and my heart shatters.
No one knows how I feel,
I cannot tell, I have a fear to reveal.

Would they judge me for my feelings?
I tried to resist, but I'm not immune to his dealings.
I know its wrong, and that's why it hurts.
I should have ignored all those idle flirts.

I need a shoulder to cry on, but there's no one there…
I don't need comments on something that I am quite aware.
I need someone to talk to…to relate to.
But there are none…not a few.

I love you,
Through and through.
It hurts
When I hear you talk about him, I revert.
He's wonderful. Fine.

I understand I have nothing to offer over him.
I understand I don't stand out in the slur.
But I can't help how I feel.
I don't even know if what I feel is real.

I must be invisible to all…
No one there to catch me when I fall.
I have plenty of friends that seem willing…
But you my friend, don't. Isn't that just thrilling?

I wish I was brave.
I wish I was smart.
I would've admitted my feelings before you went out.

I wish there wasn't,
A history between you.
He doesn't.
I don't think you do.

I need you, or someone to acknowledge me.
I need…just to be free.
I want to get through this,
This noncommittal, hypocritical, bliss.

I wish you saw me the way I do you,
It hurts me when you appear to see right through.
You hurt and don't say anything,
That scares me more than everything.

You say things jokingly, just as I do.
You don't mean to hurt me, nor I you.
Do I hurt you? It hurts me.
I shouldn't let it bother me, but I can't flee.

I should go before this gets any longer,
Just know that I will love you, hopefully…it will make me stronger.

7. Nips Of Fire

You set my soul on fire,
until I'm burning with desire.
You light the match that inspires
red-hot fantasies of you and me,
together as two lovers should be.

I'm intoxicated by your scalding touch,
and I never knew I could hunger so much.
You move my heart
like a fine work of art,
but you fuel my soul
until the fire rages out of control,
and I'm lost to fantasies of you and me,
together as two lovers should be.

I need to feel your heat,
and lose myself to kisses so sweet.
This lonely heart cries out for you,
begging for a rendezvous.
I'll get no rest until I can still,
a passion that remains volatile
from red-hot fantasies of you and me,
together as two lovers should be.

I know our spark could never miss,
when I draw fire from your kiss
and consume your body with fiery nips of delight
that each hold a promise to ignite.
Please say that you'll be mine
and cling to me as a flaming vine.

8. Why God Gave Us Friends?

God knows that everyone needs
companionship and cheer,
He knew that people need someone
whose thoughts are always near.

He knew they need someone kind
to lend a helping hand.
Someone to gladly take the time
to care and understand.

God knew that we all need someone
to share each happy day,
to be a source of courage
when troubles come our way.

Someone to be true to us,
whether near or far apart.
Someone whose love we will always
hold and treasure in our hearts.
That's why God gave us Friends!

9. On A Day Like Today

On a day like today, two lovers will meet
They'll be happy to say "you make me complete"
He'll smile and he'll laugh, and hold me tight
Then we'll go home, make love all through the night
His dad will walk down the aisle and give him away
We'll be happy in love, on a day like today

Just an ordinary day
Don't mean nothing to me
It could be in May
Or in January
He'll say all the things
I wish I could say
He'll fall in love again
On a day like today

On a day like today, he said goodbye for good
I said "I still love you dear," did all that I could
Tried to win him back, but it wasn't to be
Said he couldn't be happy with me
I tried everything, till there was nothing to say
And I lost his love, on a day like today

September third two thousand eight
I woke up alone on a regular day

It was hard to live with him going away
I stopped living my life, on a day like today!

10. A Friend Like You!

There's a lot of things
with which I'm blessed.
Though my life has been both sunny and blue
but of all my blessings,
this one's the best:
"To have a friend like you".

In times of trouble
friends will say,
"Just ask...I'll help you through it".
But you don't wait for me to ask,
you just get up and you do it.

And I can't think
of nothing in life
that I could more wisely do,
than know a friend,
and be a friend,
and love a friend...like you!

11. Love Is…

Love is the feeling I get
when I'm with you,
a desire to wrap you in my arms and
never let you go.

Love is the flutter in my chest
when you're near,
the dreamy look in my eyes
when I think of you.
Love is the emptiness
I feel when we're apart.
Day becomes night
without your bright light.
Love lasts forever -
it never fades away but only grows
stronger with each passing day.

Love is a marriage of two hearts
and two souls.
Love never grows tired;
it never grows old or weary,
but becomes ever more treasured
as the years pass
like antique lace.

12. Lush Strawberries

You're as delectable
as lush, ripe strawberries.
You're sweet from your
head to your toes,
and I want to kiss and savor
every inch of you.
I want to hold you
close to me and never
let you go!
I crave you.
I want you.
I need you.
And tonight,
after we share
some strawberries,
I intend to make
love our dessert.
So hurry home--
strawberries are
on the menu tonight.
And don't forget to bring
A bottle of whipped cream

13. Sorry, My Love…

My dear love,
I'm sorry.
I hope that you can forgive me,
and open your heart to me again.
I love you still.
I need you in my life,
and I always will.
From the bottom of my heart,
I regret what I said.
What can I do to make
things up to you?
How can I turn red
a heart I've made blue?
I only know that you
hold the key to my heart,
my happiness,
and I don't want this
great thing we have
to fall apart.
I never want to say goodbye.
I want to end this strife,
and be your lover and
best friend for the rest
Of my life

14. The Glory Of Friendship

Friendship happens when,
one person reaches out to another,
trusts, comforts, believes in that person,
hopes the best for that person, and makes
a special difference that no one else
can make

Someone who's kind and thoughtful,
whose company's a pleasure in itself?
someone who listens and understands,
whose good advice you treasure
Someone whose warmth and patience
never seems to have an end,
someone who has a loving and
a caring heart,
that someone is a FRIEND!!!

The value of a special friend cannot be measured, but only treasured!

15. When Lovers

Between a lover is exchanged many things
smiles, kisses, hugs and games.
New lives, new hopes, so much love,
a descending spiral of loving dove.

The past and future
all become one
when lovers meet
under the sun
and emotions jump
and sparks fly
when lovers meet in the night.

When lovers do the ultimate thing
and join together to make a life
and lovers kiss, not just a fling
they do this during day or night.

When lovers hold hands during sunsets
and he bends on his knee with a ring in his hand
and says the words that make the love true,
"Will you marry me, I love you..."

When lovers grow old and remain together
support each other through any weather
having made the vows and had the kiss
lovers live in total bliss.

When lovers fight and disagree
the love remains underneath
the love is true, it will fly
a real emotion never dies.

When lovers come back and trust again
and hold each other through thick and thin
and understand the emotions true
"You love me and I love you..."

When lovers sit in rocking chairs
remembering things that were there
their first kiss, and their first date
the perfume he wore while they ate.

Both of them are holding hands
wedding rings and wedding bands
and thoughts that fly, their lives do flash
the lovers die in each other's grasp.

16. Tempest Unleashed

I thought about you,
craving your silken touch.
I was shaking,
fever raging
from my desire for you.
I imagined your lips,
delicious and warm,
and my body trembled,
unsated,
needing your touch.
From my window,
there was a speck of a blood red moon,
which only served to remind me of you.
I closed my eyes,
needing rest,
yet I thought of you still.
My desire won out.
I could taste you on my lips.
I was dreaming while awake,
hungering for your kiss,
recalling images of fingers
exploring hidden places.
The passionate nights fled
without a visible trace,

but left a trail of fire.

And still I thought about you,
pressing gently into me,
wanting my satin touch,
the brush of your hair against my neck,
a mere feather like caress across my flesh,
yet a tempest unleashed.

17. Goodbye!

As I walk away
forever
from the home
we loved so much,
I lose myself
in many
memories --
that now
will reside
in my heart.

Our ghosts
will stay behind
under dancing
silver stars,
orange moons,
ethereal dawns
reflected in my calm
beloved lake,
caressed
by gentle breezes
and palm trees.

The course of life
cannot change,

evidently
I must resign,
embrace with hope
what's to come,
and bid to the past,

Goodbye!

18. Picture Of You

Memories frozen in time,

that smile forever on your face.

I stand here and focus on a picture of you,

no one could ever take your place.

When you left, I lost a part of me,

now I'm left with a picture of you.

This picture on paper as well in my mind,

a picture whose colors are still so true.

I can't deny that I miss you,

but I'm slowly letting you go.

There are times when I allow myself to look back,

at memories, for which, there's nothing tangible to show.

I will always need you,

in the same way that you need me.

But it's ok now for me to let go of the love,

that I know could never be.

I will always have my memories,

and in my mind that picture of you.

A part of me will love you forever,

but that's something I always knew.

I must've dived in without looking,

you weren't there to catch my fall.

You walked away, not looking back,

you didn't realize that you had it all.

And still I love you after all you've done,

still, I think of you every day.
I still have that picture of you in my heart,
the very picture that will always stay.

19. Will You Remember Me?

Will you remember me when I'm gone?
Could be soon; we never know how long.
What can I give you not to forget me?
To make me your fondest memory

Are my words enough to make you care?
Fading into the past, I could not bear.
I swear my love is yours alone.
It will last, as if chiselled in stone.

Am I just a whim, a game to play?
Or, in your heart, will I always stay?
I don't want you to feel pressured or distressed,
With the love with which we've been blessed

I take my words, "I love you,"
And throw them up in a sky of blue.
There, they are carried by a jet stream,
Till brought down to you on a moonbeam.

Do they echo in your ears?
Will you hear them for years and years?
I simply ask I do not plea. Will you remember me?

20. Those Three Special Words

There are only three words,
everyone wants to be heard.

They cannot be said lightly,
In passing, to be said slightly.

They shouldn't cause panic and fear,
or used as it's what one wants to hear.

Being said to one that truly does care,
While not hurting the one who does bear.

Close enough to feel the other's breath,
to see if my words truly have any depth.

While looking only in my loved one eyes,
seeing if the words are reflected as the skies.

Only then, can I say those words to you,
~~~I love you!~~~
~~~